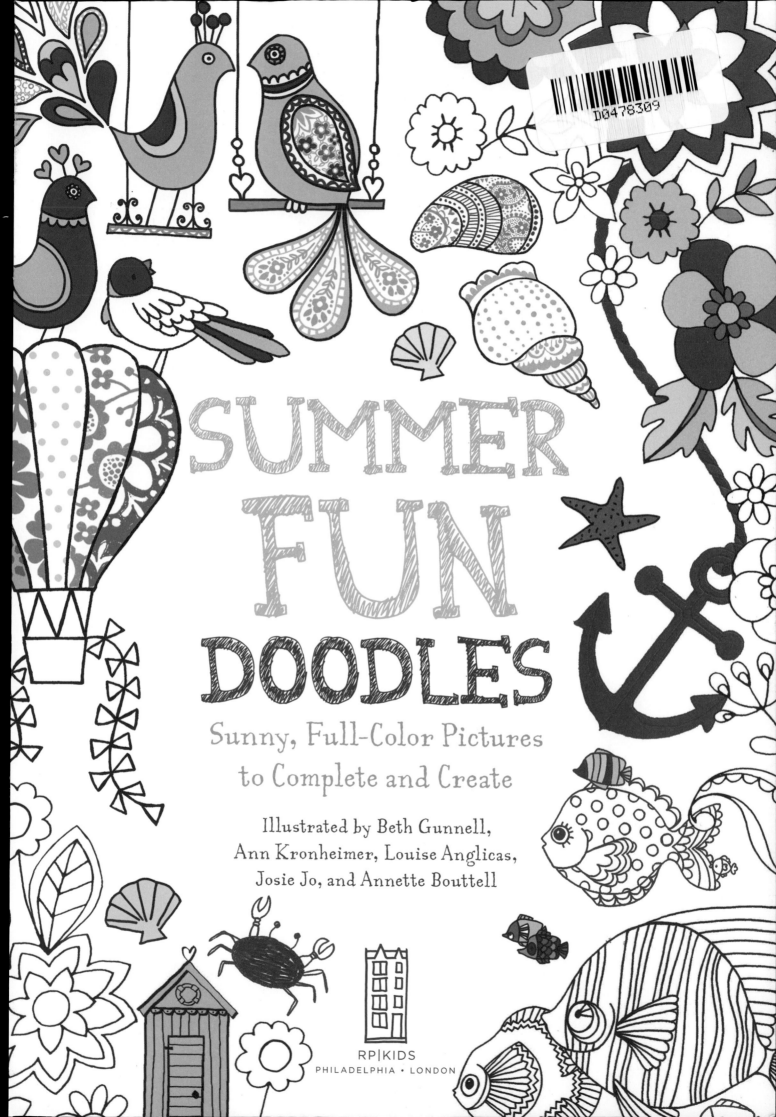

SUMMER FUN DOODLES

Sunny, Full-Color Pictures to Complete and Create

Illustrated by Beth Gunnell,
Ann Kronheimer, Louise Anglicas,
Josie Jo, and Annette Bouttell

RP|KIDS
PHILADELPHIA • LONDON

SUMMERTIME IS THE PERFECT TIME TO GET CREATIVE.

Draw sizzling designs and color with confidence,
as you complete this gorgeous book in
your own unique way.

Whether you're drawing details with a black pen
or adding vibrant color with felt-tip pens,
pencils, or crayons, it's up to you to add your signature
style to every picture.

If you are drawing on top of colored areas on the page,
leave your ink to dry for a moment to avoid smudges.

Let your creativity shine like the sun!

Copyright © 2013 by Buster Books

Illustration copyright © 2013 by Josie Jo (Folioart.co.uk). Pages: cover (crab image), 10–11, 22–23, 26–27, 38–41, 46–47, 54–55, 62–63, 79, 116–117, and 120–121. The illustration on pages 70–71 is by Julie Ingham. The illustrations on pages 86–87 and 106–107 are by Jessie Eckel.

All rights reserved under the Pan-American and International Copyright Conventions

First published in Great Britain in 2013 under the title Holiday World by Buster Books, an imprint of Michael O'Mara Books Limited, 9 Lion Yard, Tremadoc Road, London SW4 7NQ.

First published in the United States by Running Press Book Publishers, 2013

Printed in China

Books published by Running Press are available at special discounts for bulk purchases in the United States by corporations, institutions, and other organizations. For more information, please contact the Special Markets Department at the Perseus Books Group, 2300 Chestnut Street, Suite 200, Philadelphia, PA 19103, or call (800) 810-4145, ext. 5000, or e-mail special.markets@perseusbooks.com.

ISBN 978-0-7624-4901-9

9 8 7 6 5 4 3 2
Digit on the right indicates the number of this printing

Illustrated by Beth Gunnell, Ann Kronheimer, Louise Anglicas, Josie Jo, and Annette Bouttell
Edited by Sophie Schrey   Designed by Zoe Bradley

This edition published by:
Running Press Kids
An Imprint of Running Press Book Publishers
A Member of the Perseus Books Group
2300 Chestnut Street
Philadelphia, PA 19103–4371

Visit us on the web! www.runningpress.com/kids

This book was
created, colored, and
completed by

....

Complete the pretty patchwork quilt for a perfect picnic.

Finish these floaty floral maxi dresses . . .

... and complete the flowery garlands.

Totally tropical!

Use a black pen to add
fun and funky detail
to these sand castles.

Sensational seashells on the seashore.

Nice and nautical.

Be daring on deck with bold nautical patterns.

Beautiful bunting blowing in the breeze.

Make the pages burst with
bright summer flowers.

Complete the squawking, scribbly seagulls.

Complete these cool, breezy outfits for a bicycle ride.

The circus is here for the summer.

Color in the amazing acrobats.

Add more patterns to make the sun sizzle.

Make
these
beach
huts
beautiful.

Go wild with animal prints . . .

. . . and complete these kaftans with zany zebra- and daring leopard-print designs.

Beautiful birdsong fills the summer sky.

Give these girls outfits for exploring on vacation.

Add more irresistible ice creams.

Vacation scrapbook!

Make this Hawaiian pattern hot.

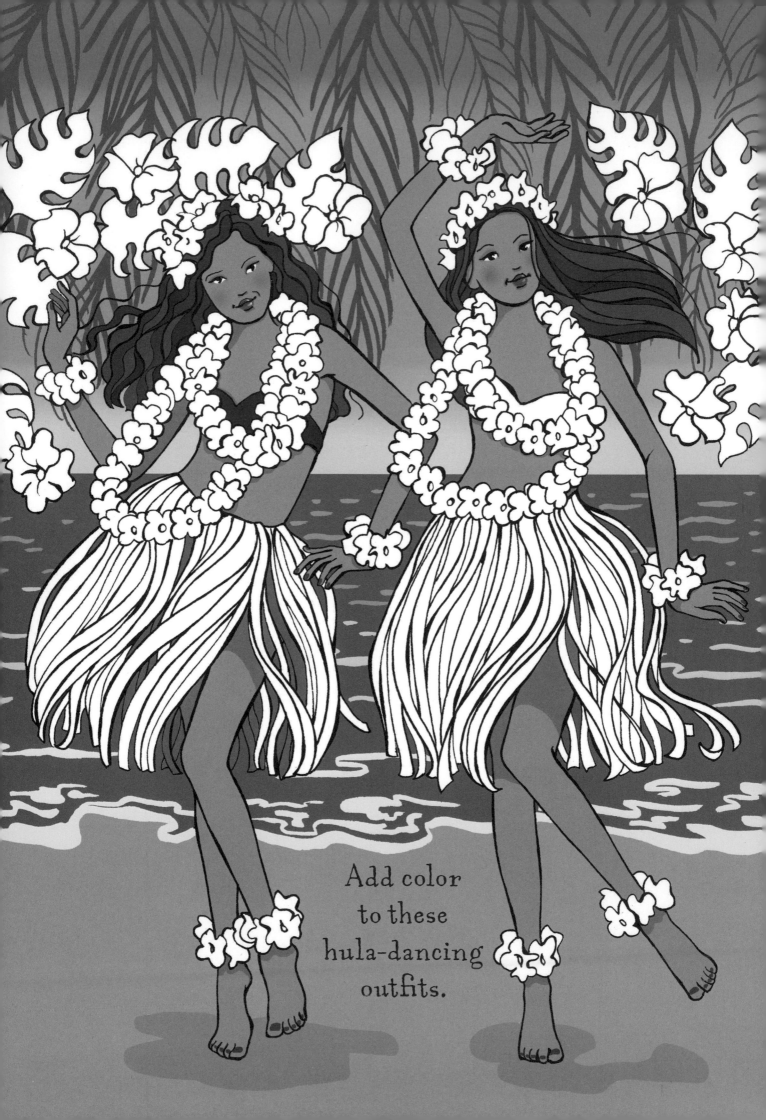

Add color
to these
hula-dancing
outfits.

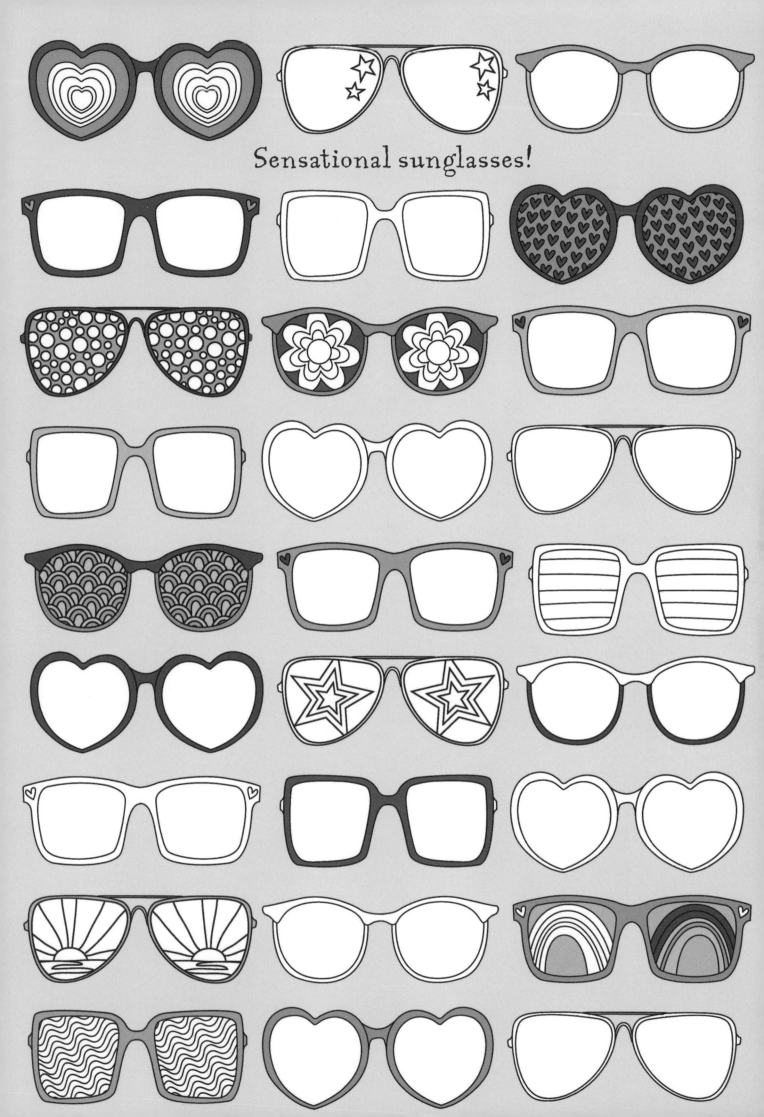

Sensational sunglasses!

Add more designs to the tents and teepees.

Complete these
funky outfits for
festival fun.

Draw more creatures under the sea.

Use a black pen to add summery silhouette shapes.

Give these beach balls bounce with bright patterns.

Make waves with show-stopping outfits, and design more headdresses.

Beautiful birds and blossoms.

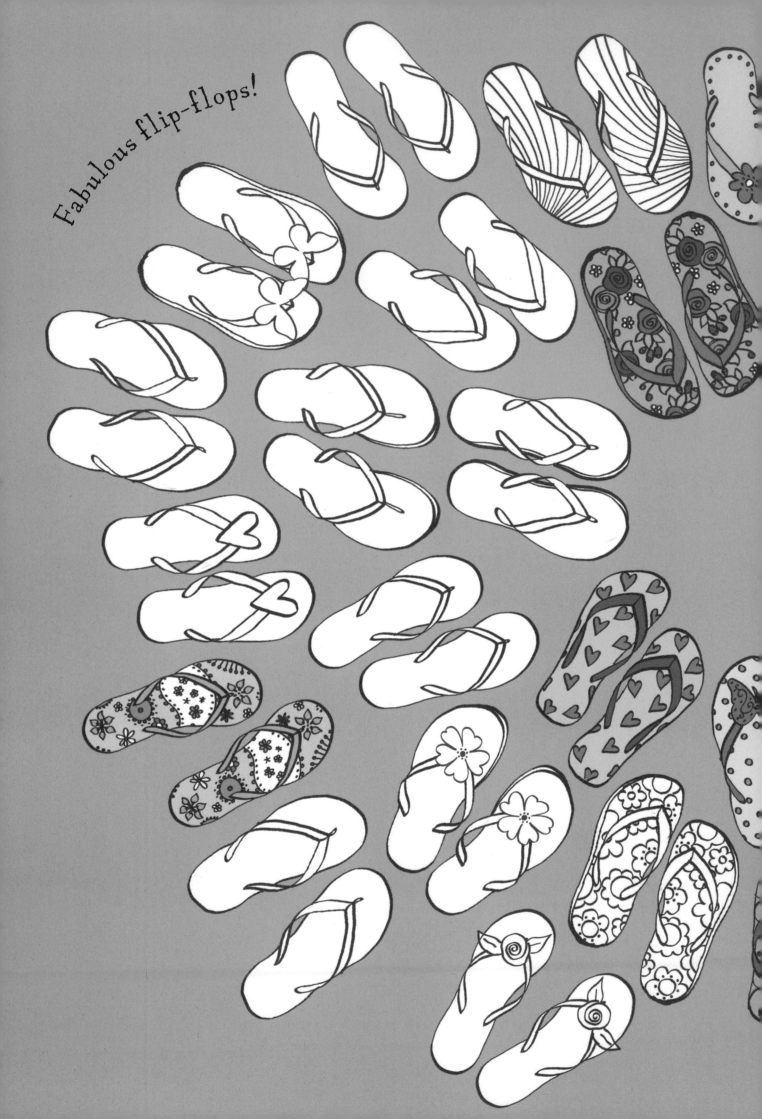

Fabulous flip-flops!

Finish these funny faces with silly sunglasses and hilarious hats and hairstyles.

Complete the bold, geometric catwalk outifts and fabric.

Add pretty patterns for a beautiful balloon ride.

Complete the vacation
souvenirs and add
more to the collection.

Summer flower power!

The fair is here for the summer.

Complete the swimwear for pool perfection . . .

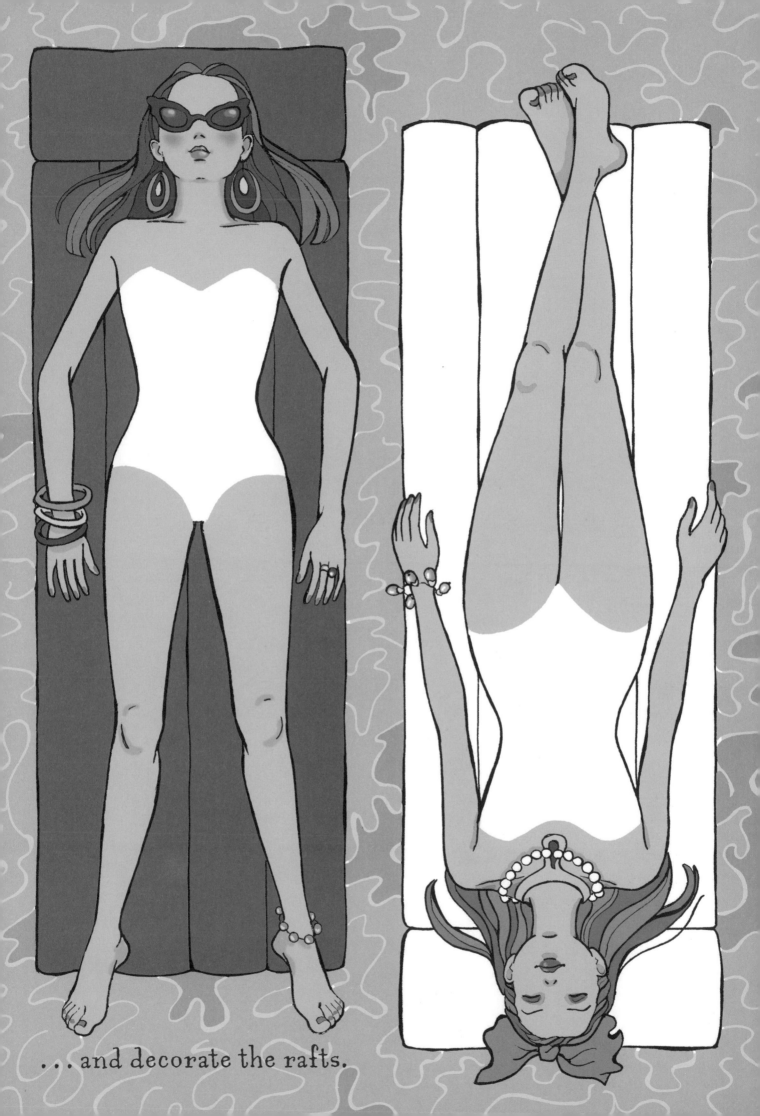

. . . and decorate the rafts.

Scatter the page with wildflowers.

Customize the luggage tags and add your destination.

Complete the ice cream vehicles in cool colors.

Sprinkle the page with more ice cream toppings.

Buckets and spades!

Add bags of style using black-line detail.

Finish the
starfish with
beautiful
colors.

Design more Mediterranean-inspired tiles.

Finish the vacation photos and add some more.

Color the Aztec-inspired pattern and complete the summer dresses.

Create
sensational
sails.

Complete pretty
parasols, perfect for
staying cool.

Add bold patterns to the 1950s swimwear.

Draw more summery hair accessories.

Make these summer dresses fabulous.

Complete the crazy, crawling creatures.

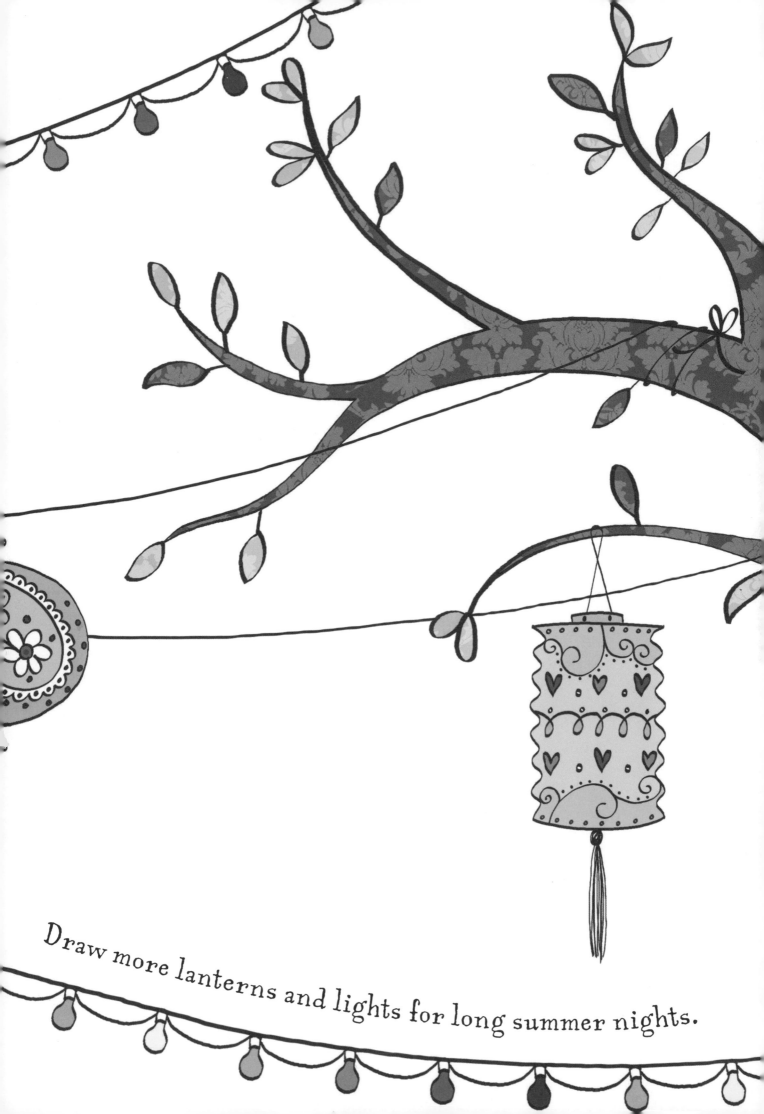

Draw more lanterns and lights for long summer nights.

Add more bright, beautiful patterns to the shell spiral.

Complete these fun outfits
for splashing around.

Color and complete these sizzling sarong fabrics.

Design cool, surfer-chick boards.

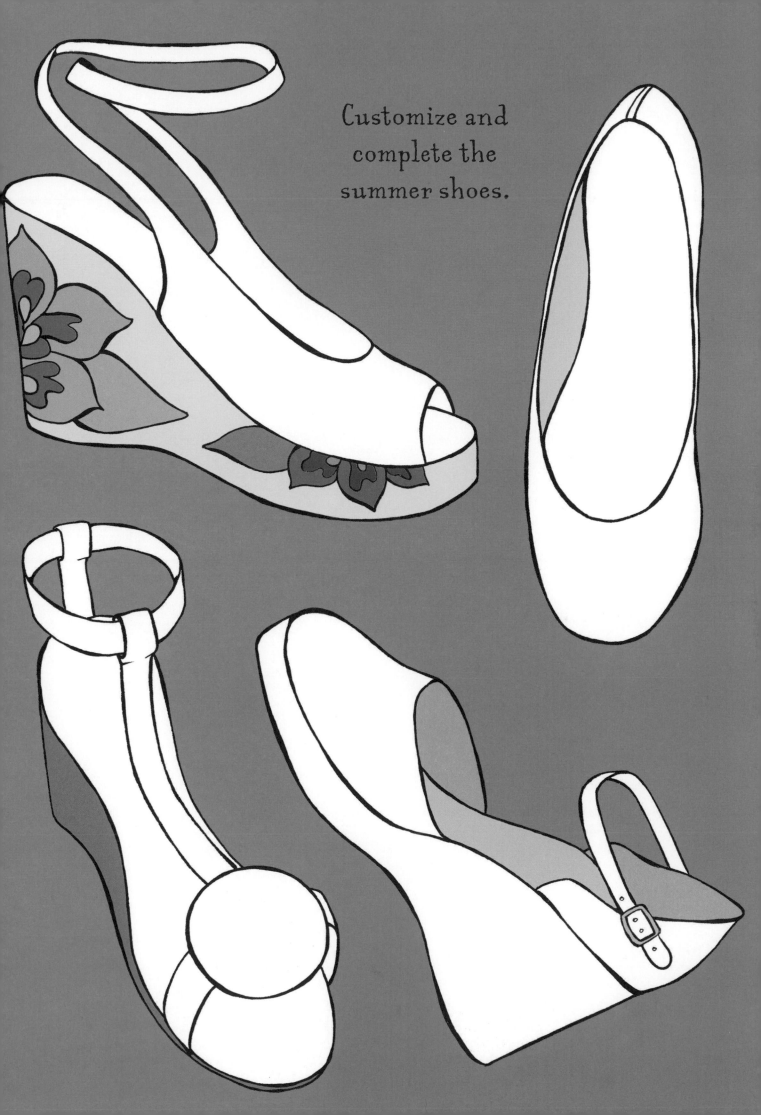

Customize and complete the summer shoes.

Design your own T-shirts and tops to take on vacation.

Add more patterns to the sun umbrellas.

Add the finishing touches to the floppy hats . . .

. . . and complete the inner tubes with really cool patterns.

Dazzling sunflowers!

Finish these fantastic fans.